WORLD WILDLIFE FUND

ISBN 0-7683-2012-7

First Printing, March 1997   Second Printing, September 1997

Published by Cedco® Publishing Company, 100 Pelican Way, San Rafael, CA 94901.
For a free catalog of our entire line of books, write us at the address above
or visit our website: *http://www.cedco.com*

front and back cover photo: © Art Wolfe
inside front cover and inside back cover photo: © Art Wolfe
title page photo: © Alan & Sandy Carey

The Panda Device and WWF are registered trademarks.
Printed in Hong Kong.

& BABIES

Mountain goat and kid

©Alan and Sandy Carey

Penguin
and
chick

©Art Wolfe

Rhinoceros and calf

Elephant and calf

Zebra and foal

Polar bear and cub

Dolphin
and calf

Buffalo and calf

©Lisa Husar

Skunk and kits

©Jeff Foott

Tiger and cub

Koala and baby

©Renée Lynn

Chimpanzee and baby

Kangaroo and joey

Moose and calf

Sea otter and pup

© Lynn M. Stone

Swan and cygnets

Cheetah and cubs

Grizzly bear and cubs

Wolf and pup

Rabbit and baby

Squirrel
and babies

©Alan and Sandy Carey

Mountain lion and cubs

Sea lion and pup

Whale and calf